Dr. D. K. Olukoya

10

Reasons,

Rules,

and

Weapons

10 REASONS, 10 RULES, 10 WEAPONS

Dr. D.K Olukoya

10 Reasons, 10 Rules, 10 Weapons
Published - August 2012
ISBN 978-0692340257

Published by: **The Battle Cry Christian Ministries**
322, Herbert Macaulay Way, Sabo, Yaba, Lagos.
P. O. Box 12272, Ikeja, Lagos.
Website: www.battlecryng.com
Email: sales@battlecryng.com
Phone: 234-803-304-4239, 01-8044415

I salute my wonderful wife, Pastor Shade, for her invaluable support in the ministry.

I appreciate her unquantifiable support in the book ministry as the cover designer, art editor and art adviser.

All scripture quotations are from the King James version of the Bible.

10 Reasons, 10 Rules, 10 Weapons
Published - August 2012
ISBN 978-0692340257

CONTENTS

Dr. D. K. Olukoya

10

Reasons,

Rules,

and

Weapons

CHAPTER ONE

10 REASONS, 10 RULES, 10 WEAPONS

Ephesians 6:12:

> *For we wrestle not against flesh and blood, but against principalities, against powers, against the rulers of the darkness of this world, against spiritual wickedness in high places.*

This chapter will acquaint you with ten reasons why a fight is inescapable, ten rules for the fight and ten serviceable weapons for victory. There are different categories of battles that we fight. There are people who should fight and when they are not doing so problems follow. Some people face a kind of battle which makes good luck elude them.

REASONS WHY YOU MUST FIGHT

1. You need to fight to possess your possessions.
2. To enlarge your coast – your present size is not your largest size. Your present position is not your final bus stop.
3. You need to fight to defend yourself and your territory.
4. To recover what the enemy has stolen from you.
5. You need to fight because you have a marching orders from heaven to fight.
6. Sometimes, when there is no war there is no peace.

7. Because there is no gentle way of arresting evil and wickedness.
8. You need to fight because the enemy as a soldier has declared war on you.
9. You need to fight, because the only language the enemy understand is violence and the only thing he respects is power.
10. You must fight to deliver yourself from bondage.

10 RULES BY WHICH TO FIGHT

1. Know your God
2. Know your enemy – it is a tragedy to fight an unknown enemy
3. Any sin in your life will strengthen your enemies
4. Know your weapons
5. In spiritual warfare, victory goes to the hardest and the meanest.
6. Utilize the hours of the night for the purposes of warfare
7. Quell your internal wars
8. Put on the whole armour of war
9. Follow the principles of operation PUSH – Pray Until Something Happens
10. Always attack by fire

10 WEAPONS TO USE IN THE FIGHT

1. Prayers that, what ought to be must be in your life must manifest by fire.
2. Prayers that make those hired to curse you wobble and stumble.
3. Prayers that make the enemy die in your place.
4. Prayers that bring down the fire of God.
5. Prayers resulting from a combination of desperate cries of holy madness.
6. Prayers for permanent arrest of arresters.
7. Holy Ghost-charged prayers that availeth much.
8. Enough is enough kind of prayers.
9. Prayers that swallow problems.
10. Prayers that scare the enemies.

PRAYER POINTS

1. Let all the weapons of captivity fashioned against me be disgraced, in the name of Jesus.
2. I decree healing and restoration to my soul, body and spirit, in the name' of Jesus.
3. I decree success, breakthrough and progress into my work, in the' name of Jesus.
4. I decree happiness, peace and fruitfulness into my undertaking, in the name of Jesus.
5. I destablise and paralyse all territorial spirits

delegated against me, in the name of Jesus.

6. Thunder and fire of God, destroy every satanic monitoring device used against me, in the name of Jesus.

7. I paralyse and destroy, all satanic embargoes placed on my progress, in the name of Jesus.

8. You evil powers, seeking my destruction, begin to fight against each other now, in the name of Jesus.

9. All havoc wrecked by impatience in my life, be repaired now, in the name of Jesus.

10. All my good prospects lost as a result of my impatience, return to me seven-fold, in the name of Jesus

11. Lord, help remove all bitterness from my heart.

12. Thou Spirit of the living God, fall afresh upon me, in Jesus' name.

13. I command every part of my body to receive spiritual correction, in the name of Jesus.

14. I disable all spiritual weapons used to slow down my progress, in the name of Jesus.

15. I cancel, all strongholds that the spirit of fear has built in me, in the name of Jesus.

16. Lord, grant me a breakthrough today, in the name of Jesus.

CHAPTER TWO

THE
INTERNAL
SHORT CIRCUIT

When I was in junior school, I was taught a song that says, "Break down every idol in your heart." I could not understand it because I thought it was not relevant to me since I was a Christian and we did not worship idols in our house. My idea of an idol was the carved head of Ogun (the Yoruba god of iron) or any other graven image. But as I matured, I began to understand what the Lord means by asking us to break down the idols in our hearts. The Bible says, *"Out of the abundance of the heart the mouth speaks"* **(Matthew 12:34).** When the heart is filled up, it would pour out through the mouth. Chatterers most of the time speak from their hearts and not from their heads. That which a person has in his heart will eventually be expressed. Sometime ago, I was counselling a couple. At a point in the process, the wife made a comment that so much infuriated the husband as to make him invoke the wrath of the god of iron upon his father-in-law.

I reacted, "But you are a Christian, why did you talk in this fashion?" He then apologized. Well, the truth is that his explosion exhibited the nature of his heart. You may try to hide but a time comes when you will be exposed. The Bible says that everything is naked before God. All fornicators and adulterers are naked before God.

13

ANGELIC VISITATION

There was a man who refused to give his life to Christ even though he was a catechist's son. One day, as he was sitting down, somebody tapped him on the shoulder and said, "You have an appointment?" He said, "Appointment?" Before he could understand what was happening, the person pulled his spirit out of his body as one would take a dress off another person. Behold, it was an angel of the living God. "Where are we going?" he asked the angel. The angel said, "Be patient, you will know very soon." Eventually, he landed before the throne of God and could not behold its glory. God called him by his name and told him that he was 25 years behind in the schedule of what He wanted him to do for Him. God said to him, "Before I go further, let us look at a review of your life." And all of a sudden, there was something like a television set and the brother was watching his life right from the moment his mother gave birth to him. He saw all the funny love letters he had written, all the fornication he had committed, all the abortions he sponsored or encouraged, etc. Everything was so clear. After he had watched to a point, he begged God to turn it off for he could not stand it any longer. That experience changed the man's life.

IDOLS IN THE HEART

Any person or thing that replaces God in your heart has become an idol. Anything you place before God or side by side Him is your idol. The moment the devotion you normally accord God is now given to any other thing or person, that substitute becomes your idol. A lot of Christians have secret idols in their hearts which put them in trouble. At this juncture, I would like you to close your eyes, lay your right hand on your chest and pray like this: "O Lord, show me the idols in my heart, in the name of Jesus."

When some people come to see a man of God, they forget that it is not every time God has a message for them. They would want to force the man of God to concoct a vision for them. Sometimes when you pray with such people and tell them that God says everything is fine, they may go but they do not believe because they have idols in their hearts.

In Ezekieal 14:4, the Lord declares:

Should I be enquired of it all by them? Therefore speak unto them, and say unto them, Thus saith the Lord God; Every man of the house of Israel that set up his idols in his heart, and pulleth the stumbling block of his iniquity before his face, and cometh to the prophet; I the Lord will answer him that

15

cometh according to the multitude of his idols.

Ezekiel 14:9-10

And if the prophet be deceived when he hath spoken a thing. I the Lord have deceived that prophet, and I will stretch out my hands upon him, and will destroy him from the midst of my people Israel. And they shall bear the punishment of their iniquity; the punishment of the prophet shall be even as the punishment of him that seeketh unto him.

The elders of Israel came to the man of God to enquire of the Lord. You would have thought that a person who needed to see a prophet would have done so with a neutral heart, but the elders approached the man of God with idols in their hearts and because of this tendency, the Lord said the reply they would get would satisfy the idols pre-enthroned in their hearts. That is, if anyone has an idol inside his heart, and he goes to a prophet for information, God would ask that prophet to answer him according to the idol in his heart and the person ends up getting the wrong information.

Many people have secret idols hidden in the chambers of their hearts from the sight of men but not God. These idols decide sometimes what they get from God. **Hebrews 4:13:** Neither is there any creature that is not manifest in his sight but all things are naked and opened unto the eyes of him with whom we have to do." So, all the things people try to hide are open before God.

WHEN PRAYER BOUNCES

Sometime ago, a man and a woman came to see me. The woman requested me to help the man, that his enemies were destroying him. As I started praying it was as if my prayers were bouncing back to me. I stopped and asked the woman to go out. After she had left, I asked the man of her identity, and he said she was just somebody who was concerned about his situation I asked if that was all and he answered "yes." I asked him to go too. Later, they came back and the man said "Please, sir, forgive me I can see that it is not good to tell lies to a man of God. That woman is supposed to be my fourth wife. I am just planning to marry her." This testimony confirms what the bible says that the Lord will answer them according to the idols in their hearts.

A good number of singles have already made up their minds concerning the type of partners they would like to

17

have before praying to God to show them who to marry. As a result, they find it difficult to accept God's will for their lives. God eventually gives them the idols they crave for. Pray this prayer point: "O Lord, deliver me from secret idols, in the name of Jesus."

SILLY PRETENCE

If you are a committed Bible student, you will find that there was a man whom the bible castigates. His name is Jeroboam the son of Nebat. The Bible describes anybody that committed a serious offence as Jeroboam the son of Nebat. He became an evil yardstick. What was his offence? He set up an idol in Dan and another one in Bethel and called the people of Israel together and said, "You house of Israel, behold the god that delivered thee from the land of Egypt." But wait, before Jeroboam started installing the physical idols, the germ of idolatry first prospered in his heart. Along the line, however, something happened: Jeroboam's son became sick and because Jeroboam had spurned God he was not aware that the prophet in Israel was already blind. He told his wife to take the child to him and find out whether the son would live or not. He also asked her to disguise herself so as to evade recognition - human craft! As the wife of Jeroboam, now got up as someone else, reached the blind prophet's doorstep and knocked, his voice rang out:

18

"Come thou in, you wife of Jeroboam, why frameth thyself to be another?" (that is why are you pretending to be another person?) Before she could open the door, the prophet went further to tell her why she was visiting.

Many people who come to church find it difficult to fit into any group because none of the groups is ready to admit those who still "paint" their faces. Such people keep running around just because of an idol. If the Lord tells you to serve Him in an area with a condition attached to it and you do not want to abide by the condition, you are saying in effect that you have another god.

Those who find it difficult to put away their false finger nails, attachments and make-ups need deliverance because those things have become idols in their lives. Beloved, think about these things seriously.

When God gave Saul an instruction, he carried it out in his own way and Samuel told him, "Behold, obedience is better than sacrifice and to hearken than the fat of ram." He was also told that rebellion is as the sin of witchcraft and stubbornness is as iniquity and idolatry. **(I Samuel 15:22-23)** implying that a witch and a rebellious person are twin brothers heading for hell fire. A stubborn person and an idol worshipper are the same before God.

Nowadays, we have a lot of idols that people worship.

They include the following:

1. **Money:** A lot of people now just keep running after money all the time. They do not understand any other language except money. When you tell them to get serious with the Lord, they would say, "I will become very serious with the Lord when I make my first million." When you ask them to come to night vigils, they will tell you that they must work overtime to make ends meet. They do not know that the only person that can help make ends meet is the Lord Jesus. I know a man who had a small boil on his neck that cost him more than half of his salary to treat. So, at the end of the day, it is only God that can bolster up your finances. "Seek ye first the kingdom of God and all other things shall be added unto you," the Bible says. But when you start seeking all other things before the kingdom, you have an idol in your heart. The Bible says, "I have been young, and now am old; yet have I not seen the righteous forsaken nor his seed begging bread." There was no man who sought the kingdom of God and got it that ever remained poor. What is the use of gathering money and at the end of the day you go to hell fire? What is the use of gathering money and at the end of the day, some people are just waiting for you to die so that they can

fight and devour each other over the wealth they did not help create?

2. **The world:** There are so many fellowships now where all they talk about is financial prosperity. According to them, if you are a herbalist, a thief, or a fornicator, God will prosper you. They say, "Come whoever you are and donate money."

3. **Fame:** A lot of people lust for popularity. They just want to be known without realizing that if the whole world knows you and God does not know you, you are wasting your time.

4. **Pleasure:** People just want to relax and enjoy themselves.

5. **Power:** Some people are desperately seeking political and religious power. They can do anything to acquire them.

6. **Knowledge:** Some people have turned their certificates to their god. God hates idolatry with a perfect hatred. Once you give what is due to God to an object, special demons move in and turn that thing into something powerful. The internal idols will then

invite wicked spirits from outside. Until these internal idols are destroyed, you cannot make a headway as a Christian.

SECRET IDOLS

Let us look at the secret idols that many Christians are carrying around. You will do yourself a lot of good to look deeply into your spirit because these may be the things that the enemy is using to deal with you whereas you think it is witches or wizards that are harassing you.

1. **Unforgiveness:** This is common amongst Christians. Many Christians harbour malice against fellow believers. If you as a christian are at odds with your neighbours in the same compound, not because of your faith but on account of your failure to perform some common chores or observe some agreed rules of cleanliness, I am afraid, you have an idol in your life. It is no use trying to justify yourself. Let it be emphasized that an unforgiving attitude is a terrible idol. Some people cannot forgive their pastors, group leaders, university lecturers, etc. Don't forget that anytime you come to God with an idol in your heart, the first thing that the enemy would say is, "O God, hold on, look at this." And the unforgiving idol will say, "I am here, sir."

I can still remember, a woman came to me for prayers years back. She complained that things were rough and her business was grounded. As I was praying, the Lord said, "Son, there is somebody this woman does not want to forgive." I opened my eyes and said, "Madam there is somebody you do not want to forgive. God says you should first of all forgive that person before any other thing." She looked at me and said it was her husband. I asked her to forgive him. She said "no," that the man had hurt her badly. She said when they were poor and struggling, the man did not abandon her. But when they became rich, the man went and married a girl of the age of their last daughter as second wife and abandoned her. So she would not forgive him. I told her that the Bible says she must forgive him no matter what he had done. She went away in anger because I refused to pray for her. But the next day, she came back and said she was ready to forgive him. After she repented and forgave the man and we prayed, all the miracles that she had been asking for, for five years came within a week and since then her economic life has improved dramatically.

2. **Bitterness.**

3. **Jealousy.**

4. **Envy.**

5. **Hatred:** Unforgiveness, bitterness, jealousy and envy give birth to hatred. The existence of these vices invariably begets hatred in a person's heart. And any believer that nurses hatred against anybody and who does not repent will go to hell fire.

6. **Discouragement:** Many people get easily discouraged. They lose hope when their prayers are not answered quickly or when they are disappointed. In a vision, a sister was shown the shop of the devil. In it, she saw hypertension, diabetes, bad luck and all other health conditions with their price tags. She asked the devil, "Mr. Devil, which is the most expensive item in your store?" The devil told her it was discouragement. He told her that once he was able to get believers discouraged, he would capture them. She asked agaim, "When does discouragement come to a person?" He explained to her that discouragement sets in after depression and both of them give birth to hopelessness. Sometimes when a

Christian is heading for a miracle and the devil desires to hinder the breakthrough, he uses discouragement.

7. **Worry:** The reason why some people are looking older than their age is that they entertain worry. They groan over little things.

8. **Confusion:** Confusion gives birth to fear. This is present in many lives and is an idol. It must be cast out today.

9. **Impatience:** Impatience is the opposite of patience. Patience is a virtue. The patient person always laughs last. But the impatient person will spoil the blessing that God has for him. The perfect wife or husband is the one who agrees that he or she is not married to a perfect partner.

10. **Selfishness.**

11. **Evil thoughts:** These give birth to evil imaginations. Many Christians commit sins in their hearts. No serious Christian will bow down to physically carved idols but they worship the idols in their hearts. You see believers watching unedifying films which they are supposed to shun because some idol

lurks in their hearts.

12. **Doubt.** Many believers are doubters like Thomas who said, "Well I am a honest doubter. I am not asking for too much. All I am saying is let Jesus come and show me His hand because I saw Him when He died on the cross and I was there when He was buried. Now you say He has resurrected. I will also like to touch the holes in His hands and feet because the holes cannot heal within three days." So, when Jesus got there, He said, "Thomas it is because you have seen me that is why you believe. But blessed are those who have not seen me and yet they believe." Those simple words changed him. He died preaching the gospel. Doubt is an idol and the Bible says a doubting man is like the wave of the sea. Such a person does not believe that he can receive anything from the Lord. Some people have high level of doubt. Such people even ask if there is God at all. Some people doubt so much that they do not even believe that witches exist.

13. **Indecision.** This is another idol which has destroyed so many people.

14. **Pride.** Pride leads to self-exaltation and unteachable spirit.

All these secret idols must be chased out by the Lion of Judah. The problem of the idol is that it hinders the move of God. God is saying, "Clear away the idols. Cast them into the fire. Then you will see what I can do." There was a medical doctor whose death provoked his wife to pray so desperately for hours for him to be raised. Eventually the man came back to life and narrated what he saw. He saw himself arriving in a place where somebody held him by the right hand and another person held him by the left hand and they were dragging him away. He first of all thought that they were taking him to heaven but as they dragged him along, he felt heat on his face. He remembered the Bible and reasoned: "If this place is heaven the breeze will not be uncomfortable." Then he began to appeal to them to leave him alone. He told them he was born again and that they should not whisk him to hell fire. They did not listen. As they hurled him to the edge of hell fire, he saw people being dumped into the lake of fire like a tipper lorry discharging sand. He was amazed and suddenly as they were about to throw him inside, a voice sounded from above, "Release him." And they left him. Immediately they released him the devil came out and said, "O God, You have no right to take this man to heaven, because he is free from all sins apart from one which is idolatry of the heart." Just one, but many of us are committing serious sins daily.

God said, "Okay, agreed" (The devil does not tell lies

against anybody. If the devil is reporting you to God, he tells God the truth. But you cannot tell God a lie anyway). God said. "Devil, you are right. I am not taking this man to heaven, because he is not qualified as you have said, but at the same time, I will not allow him to go to hell fire now because of his wife." The importunate prayers of his wife compelled God to send him back to life. Although that man was a Sunday School Teacher and he taught the Bible very well, there was an idol hidden in him.

On the last day, if an idol is still in a person apart from the idol hindering his blessing, the person cannot go to heaven. Our greatest prayer should be: "O Lord, break down every idol in our hearts, in the name of Jesus."

If you have not given your life to Jesus, and you try to remove any idol from your heart, the idol will resist you because you belong to the same camp. So, to be able to break the idols in your heart, you must give your life to Christ.

PRAYER POINTS

1. O Lord, break down every idol in my heart, in the name of Jesus.
2. I cast out, every idol from my heart, in the name of Jesus.
3. I break down, every hidden idol, in the name of

28

Jesus.

4. Let the fire of God boil all rivers harboring my enemies, in the name of Jesus.

5. Let the blood of Jesus wipe off all my evil dreams, in the name of Jesus.

6. I destroy, every satanic accident organized for my sake, in the name of Jesus.

7. Every Idol that I have been dedicated to consciously or unconsciously, release me and die, in the name of Jesus.

8. I break myself loose from every grip of any idol, in the name of Jesus.

9. Every plan of the wicked against my soul, scatter, in the name of Jesus.

10. Every wicked spirit polluting my hearts receive the stones of fire, in the name of Jesus.

11. Every warfare, prepared by wicked spirits against my life, I command spiritual acid upon you in the name of Jesus.

12. Oh God arise and scatter the camp of wicked spirit fashioned against me, in the name of Jesus.

CHAPTER THREE

MY LIFE IS NOT FOR SALE

The Bible explains that such phenomena as 'bondage,' 'freedom,' 'power,' 'anointing' etc are spiritual categories and if they are not sorted out or explicated in the appropriate spiritual fashion, one might just be labouring under serious illusions in the physical world. Real power is not in the physical world but in the spiritual world. The children of darkness understand this fact very well.

Ezekiel 13:18-19

> *Thus saith the Lord God; Woe to the women that sew pillows to all armholes and make kerchiefs upon the head of every stature to hunt souls. Will you hunt the souls of my people, and will ye save the souls alive that come unto you? And will you pollute me among my people for handfuls of barley and for pieces of bread, to slay the souls that should not die and to save the souls alive that should not live, by your lying to my people that hear your lies?*

In the foregoing, we could see an exchange taking place. The souls that are not supposed to die are being slain to save the souls that should not live. There are also some people that are destined to die but they look for the lives of younger persons, snuff them out and add them to theirs. They save alive the souls that should not live by lying to the people that hear their lies.

Verses 20-21

Wherefore thus saith the Lord God, Behold, I am against your pillows (pillows in original Hebrew means magic band), wherewith ye hunt the souls to make them fly (meaning that people can be initiated unconsciously), and I will tear them from your arms and will let the souls go even the souls that ye hunt to make them fly. Your kerchiefs also will I tear and deliver my people out of your hands and they shall be no more in your hand to be hunted and ye shall know that I am the LORD.

So, deliverance is needed to get out of their grip.

MAGIC BANDS

This is an interesting scripture. Some people are using magic bands to trap the souls of men. The souls that should normally be at rest, they make them fly. This is why when some people are asleep, they face battles. There are powers who hanker after their souls to exchange them for handfuls of barley and pieces of bread. Somebody approaches a witchdoctor and tells him, "I want to destroy this person," and he is asked to go and bring "kolanut" (a kind of nut used for ritual purposes in African societies) and a goat, which would be used to snuff out the person's soul. These are powers that engage in selling souls. That is why I declare, "My life is not for sale."

All reasonable people sell disposable things, but when a man decides to sell a non-disposable item, it means that spiritual madness has crept in. Many lives are on sale. Many are being sold now and many have been sold. There is in the spirit world what we may describe as the prostitution of the soul. That is, when the soul of a person becomes a prostitute in the spirit world, all manner of misfortune befall that hapless individual in the physical environment. There are people who complain of romantic harassment by spirit spouses in their dream. Such people may have become prostitutes in the spirit, their souls having been sold off.

Jesus says, "What shall it profit a man if he gains the whole world and loses his soul? With what can a man make exchange for his soul? Nothing.

SOULS FOR SALE

When the soul of a person is put up for sale, it is a great problem. Jesus says, "What can you give in exchange for a soul?" In Ezekiel 13, we see people exchanging souls of men for mere pieces of bread. So, the worst enemies of men are soul traders. They hunt for souls and trade with them.

Revelation 18:11 says,
> *And the merchants of the earth shall weep and mourn over her; for no man buyeth their merchandise any more.*

What is their merchandise? They are listed in

Revelation 18:12-13 which says,
> *The merchandise of gold and silver, and precious stones, and of pearls, and fine linen, and purple, and silk, and scarlet and thine wood, and all manner vessels of ivory, and all manner vessels of most precious wood, and of brass, and iron, and marble. And cinnamon, and odours, and ointments, and frankincense, and wine, and oil, and fine flour, and wheat, and beasts, and sheep, and horses, and chariots and slaves and souls of men.*

These are the merchandise of soul traders. Please, declare this to yourself, *"My life is not for sale."*

Isaiah 50:1
> *Thus saith the Lord, Where is the bill of your mother's divorcement, whom I have put away? Or which of my creditors is it to whom I have sold you? Behold, for your iniquities have ye sold yourselves, and for your transgressions is your mother put away.*

That means that, you can sell yourself consciously or unconsciously, or your parents or friends can sell you off.

Isaiah 52:3 *also says,*
> *For thus saith the Lord, Ye have sold yourselves for nought; and ye shall be redeemed without money.*

DESTINY DISORDER

When a life has been sold off, there would be destiny disorder. Several years ago, I met a sister who had this problem. Her grandmother married her off to someone in the spirit world, collected her bride price spiritually, spent it also spiritually and that grandmother was now dead. Every night, when she slept there was a short demon by her bed. She prayed against and bound and bound it all to no avail. It would disappear for a while only to reappear. When she was going to the toilet at night, it would step aside physically for her to pass. It was always there watching carefully over her anytime she was in bed. If there were other people on the bed, this possessive, jealous lover was visible only to the sister. It was the guard of the husband which her grandmother married her to in the spiritual world. Five men tried to marry her in real life but each of them ended up in disaster. The suitor who suffered the least disaster drank the water of his car battery.

Please, take the following prayer points:
- Every power, hunting for my soul, die, in the name of Jesus.
- My soul, be delivered from satanic flight, in the name of Jesus.

When a life has been sold out, there would be destiny disorder; the destiny is as good as dead. This is the major problem of the black man. Let us look at the names of some black people in the Bible:

Hagar, an Egyptian who married Abraham, Keturah who also married Abraham - Asenath who was Joseph's wife,

Ziporrah who was Moses' wife and Jethro. Moses' father-in-law who proffered some hints to Moses on how to manage people and time. Obab who piloted the Israelites in the wilderness - they were going to the Promised Land and did not quite know the way and this black man was their guide; Rahab saved the Israelite spies at Jericho. In the New Testament, there was Simon of Cyrene. When Jesus was on His way to Calvary and the cross became too heavy for Him, this man helped carry the cross to the place of Jesus' crucifixion. In the book of Jeremiah, we read about a man called Ebedmelech, an Ethiopian. There was a time that Jeremiah was thrown into the dungeon. It was this black man that brought him out. In Acts of the Apostles, we read about the Ethiopian Eunuch to whom Philip preached. When Paul was going on his missionary journey, two of the three men who laid hands on him in prayer were Lucius called Niger and Simeon of Cyrene. They were both black men.

Do you know that the gospel got to Africa before it reached Europe? Do you know that whenever God had a major step to take in history a black man somehow was involved? God has always used Africa to execute His moves. Whenever the world was in a crisis, God brought a black man to the scene. With this background, you may now ask: what exactly is wrong with the black man? Why do white men tell condescending tales about us? Why did we blacks go through the horrifying slave trade? You cannot read the story of the slave trade without crying. Men and women were gathered and packed into ships like sardines. There was no walking space and no toilet. When they fell sick, the only solution was to cast them overboard and they served as food for fishes. Why did they suffer that treatment? Why is it very difficult to find a single black nation that is doing very well? What is responsible for the demonic and diabolical attack from hell fire to stop the black man from executing his prophetic mandate? Why should things like poverty, inferiority complex, confusion, insufficient education and civil war be so rampant with blacks? This puzzle is explicable by reference to destiny disorder in the lives of individuals. When Mr. A whose destiny is in disorder marries a woman whose destiny is also in disorder, they bring forth children who inherit destiny disorder and the circle continues.

Please, pray like this: *"I refuse to enter the dustbin of life, in the name of Jesus."*

THE DUSTBIN OF LIFE

There are many human beings who are already dumped into the dustbin of life and they are weeping and crying.

Sometime ago, something happened in one city in the western part of Nigeria. It was noticed that a man had a big farm and the farm prospered. The produce from the farm was very good. But the surprising thing was that, no one had ever seen any workers on that farm, yet it was the largest farm around and belonged to one old man. This man had a son who wondered about the farm. He did not know who was planting the crops because he understood that his father was old and could not do much. As he began to cleverly study his father, he discovered that anytime he arrived at the farm, he would wash his face with a concoction. One day, the son used the concoction to wash his face and he saw the people working on the farm. They were people who had died in the village. Imagine his father's wickedness, holding down people who were dead to serve him before they go to hell. The devil had traded their souls to the old man. When they died the man bought their souls to work on his farm. The boy screamed when he saw them. Then his father knew that he had touched the concoction. He ran after him but could not catch him owing to his physical weakness. The son disappeared into the town screaming. Till now no one has seen the old man again, but the farm is still there.

If you allow your soul to be sold, it is your own business. That is why when you come to the house of God, you better face your business. Do not waste time on joking with the enemy or on things that do not concern you. If you do, your disorder will multiply. It will be a major disaster if you finish reading these lines without having a touch from heaven.

GOD'S PURPOSE

God has a purpose for everything He does. The fact that someone is walking about does not mean that the person is alive in the book of the Almighty. He may be moving about, breathing or going to church, but by God's reckoning, he might have died 20 years ago. God has a purpose for your life. Before you were born He has written certain things about your life. The enemy can see those things, therefore he can cause destiny disorder if he succeeds in grabbing your soul. So, the most precious material on planet earth is the soul of a man. The devil is after it, God too is after it. When Peter said to Jesus, "You cannot die like that, how can you die?" He looked at Peter and said, "The Son of man goeth as it is written of Him." Something was written about you. Is that thing in disorder now? If it is in disorder, then the soul traders have done their worst.

Sometime in the past, a woman gave birth and somebody visited her at the maternity. She gave her baby to the visitor while she went to the toilet. Shortly afterwards, another visitor came in. As she was in the toilet, she overheard her two visitors arguing and wondered what the matter was but immediately she got back to the room, a hush descended. Now suspicious and combative, she thundered, "If two of you do not tell me what you were discussing, somebody must die here today." Then one of them said, "When I got here, my friend had already removed four and she wanted to remove the other three. So, all I was saying is that she should leave the other three for me." They were referring to the stars on the head of the newly born baby. This is a specie of wickedness going on in the world.

YOUR EARTHLY PURPOSE

Life become pointless, if it does not fulfil its divine destiny. Once your soul has been sold off, unless it is bought back, you may not be able to fulfill the destiny that the Lord has for you. For several years, I taught biology in a secondary school and in an adult education school where the youngest person in my class was 36 years old. One day, I discussed amoeba for three hours. After the lecture, I said, "Any question?" A bald headed man at the middle said he had a question. He said, "During the wedding of amoeba who collects the dowry?" I was shocked because his query revealed that he did not understand anything out of all I had said for three hours.

The trouble with that fellow was that he was doing the right thing at the wrong time. It is destiny disorder. He might have been interested in going to school at the appropriate time but couldn't because witches had 'eaten up' the money of all those who would have financed his education. He might have had the brain but was unable to go to school. His destiny was in a mess.

Nahum 3:3 says:

> *The horsemen lifteth up both the bright sword and glittering spear: and there is a multitude of slain, and a great number of carcasses, and there is none end of their corpses, they stumble upon their corpses.*

Why the pile of corpses?
Verse 4 volunteers:

> *Because of the multitude of the whoredom of the well-favoured harlot, the mistress of witchcrafts, that selleth nations through her whoredom and families through her witchcrafts.*

SOUL TRADERS

1. **Witchcraft Powers:** The first major sellers of souls are witchcraft powers. We can see where their

activities have led the black man today. Unfortunately, they have wangled their way into many churches. In fact, in many places today, it is mostly the witches who say, "Thus says the Lord." And many people go to them for prayers out of ignorance. Most times in their prayers, it is only names like 'Olodumare', 'Osanobua', 'Chineke' that would be mentioned. They do not mention the name, Jesus.

When man fell in the Garden of Eden, the religion he turned to was witchcraft because rebellion was the cause of his fall. Rebellion is as the sin of witchcraft. I used to think that Taiye and Kehinde (twins) love each other until I met a Kehinde who told me that she had put the life of her twin sister on the shelf, that until she had married and had three or four children, then would the other lady taste matrimony. Both of them came from the same womb but look at the evil that witchcraft can do. We need to be aggressive, if we do not want soul traders to sell us off. A lot of people have been sold already so they do not understand what is going on. Perhaps you have been sold already and do not know. During the slave trade, villages were invaded, people were captured and whisked away.

43

It is often said that the people who are looking are very many, but the people who see are very few. The greatest enemy of man is not without but within. Unless the internal defeat is registered, external defeat can never come. Unfortunately, many people who come to the house of God do not possess this ability to see. There is need to pray the prayer of Elisha who said to his servant, "Brother, do not worry, those who are with us are more than those who are with them." And straight away, the servant could see two armies - the hosts of the Lord and the enemy troops.

The foundation of spiritual failure that the modern man is experiencing is spiritual blindness. A person has been sold but he does not know. A person has been thrown into jail but he does not know. A person is wearing a three-piece suit and is studying for Ph.D. in the university but already he has been sold. Evil birds have eaten up the good seed planted in many lives. For instance, do you know the real life you are supposed to be living? Many people do not know. Have your enemies converted you to a hewer of wood and drawer of water? Look at yourself. Is your real life dead or alive?

Have your dreams and visions been extinguished?

44

Are you dead whilst still alive? Is there anything that makes you accept an inferior or disabled life as your life? Is there anything that keeps you permanently depressed and unhappy? Are you deceiving yourself by having a form of godliness but denying the power thereof? Are you the type of person who x-rays a man or woman in the laboratory of your heart?

Perhaps you are not who you should be now. The real life of many people exist only in the dream. They count money in the dream but they live in penury in real life. They own companies only in the dream but are jobless here. They preach to thousands of people in the dream but are powerless here. They live in houses in the dream but here they have three quit notices.

There is something you must destroy today. You must refuse to be caged or boxed in by the enemy. You must refuse to accept the satanic substitute for your destiny. You must pray and get your unused things, and your buried Lazarus must resurrect. You must renounce the curse of powerless living. You must disallow the enemy from dulling the edge of your sword. You must disallow the enemy from closing down the factory of your life. You must refuse the call from the camp of the enemy that you should drop your weapon.

2. **The second means through which souls are sold is prophetic manipulation:** This is where many people make mistakes. That is why the Mountain of Fire and Miracles Ministries is a do it yourself church. It is not a place where "the man of God must pray for me" syndrome flourishes. No. It is a "do it yourself" place. When people surrender the totality of themselves to the prophet, they are looking for destiny disorder because when God does not give a message and you ask the prophet, "What do you see?" he may give you an information that is not from God. The work of a man of God calls for a high sense of responsibility. Men of God therefore have to be very careful.

The devil knows that people believe their pastors and would do whatever they ask them to do, so he looks for his men and pushes them into the position of fake men of God who give people demonically inspired prophecies to confuse them. Sometimes, parents go to the fake prophets behind the back of their children to ask the prophets to convince the children to do what they want. For example, a parent could go to such a prophet and say, "Prophet, there is one fine man coming to see our daughter but we don't know what is wrong with the girl, she is chasing away the man. What we want you to do is to call her and tell her that the man is her husband." The prophet would then call the girl and say to her: "Is there anyone coming to visit you at home? That person is your husband." He says this without prayer or revelation. The sister too is not given time to pray. That way, her destiny is put in disorder.

Several years ago, a pregnant sister going to the market met a white garment prophet who said, "Thus says the Lord: Unless you bring this or that you will die with this pregnancy." She held on to his clothes and said, "You must reverse what you have said if not, you will not leave this place." People started gathering and saying, "Sister, leave the man of God alone." She told them what he said and insisted that they should ask him to reverse it. The people now said, "Why did you deliver such a message to the woman?. Reverse it quickly." Then he said, "You will deliver safely," etc.

Again, years back, another sister came and said that a prophet in her mother's church told her that she would die, that I should pray for her and cancel it. I said, "No. You go back and tell the prophet that your pastor said, I should tell you that you will die." She went and the prophet did not last beyond the following seven days. The arrow of death went back to its sender. The devil has a way of gluing one's mind to evil prophecies. If you know that evil prophecies have been uttered against you by astrologers, unholy prophets, herbalists or that any ungodly person has foretold your future, pray this prayer point aggressively: Every satanic programme for my destiny, die, in the name of Jesus.

3. **Joining yourself to a harlot:** If you sleep with a man or woman outside marriage, you introduce disorder into your life. The Bible tells us that, you become one with a sex partner. If you have gone with up to 30 to 40 men or women, it means that your life has been fragmented into pieces. You need to pray. The destiny of Samson was reversed because of this. The way he ended up was not God's plan for his life. It was a plan of the powers of wickedness. A man who sleeps with a married or single woman outside marriage is digging his own grave. You may think you are enjoying yourself. No. You are putting your life in disarray.

4. **Contamination from the womb:** This is the reason why pregnant women have to be careful of where they go. Drinking concoctions, attaching strange things to your dresses, paying aimless and useless

visits and consumption of demonic food will cause destiny disorder.

5. **Idol worship:** God hates idol worship with perfect hatred. If you check your name and find a hint of idol worship about it, that indicates that destiny disorder looms. You must sever every link with idolatry.

6. **Anger:** Anger can manifest itself in several ways. It may be in shouting, slamming the door, in using abusive language, pounding on the tables or the ground, throwing objects at people or destroying objects. It may be in the form of fighting, acrimonious arguments or negative and critical comments. Anger may reflect in a scowl, hissing, hatred, depression or murder. Anyone in the grip of the spirit of anger is liable to put his destiny in disorder. Anger will control that person if it is not controlled. It hamstrings or constrains spiritual holy living. Angry people normally have retarded spiritual growth. They quarrel often and so cannot pray effectively. Angry people have bad testimony. It saps their ability to serve the Lord.

7. **Household wickedness:** There are many examples of this in the Bible. Jesus told us in **Matthew 10:36** that the enemies of a man shall be members of his own household. Eve was used by the devil against

Adam. Cain was used against Abel, Lot against Abraham and Jacob against Esau. Joseph's brethren dealt with him. Miriam, Moses' sister who took Moses out of the river was against him. Absalom overthrew his father. Judas Iscariot, one of Jesus' 12 disciples, the treasurer of the church, eventually betrayed his Master.

We need to pray, not the type of prayer the enemy will hear and rejoice. The first thing we need to do is to repent of all transgressions that gave the enemy the chance to sell our souls or tamper with our lives. We need to ask God to forgive us, so that we can start moving forward. After asking for forgiveness, we will move on and identify the disorder and then call God into our situation. It will be a tragedy, after reading this message you do not receive the touch of God. The Bible says, "The Son of man goeth as it is written." Are you going as God has written of you, or you are going as your enemy has written? Or are you going according to verdict of witchcraft? You have the opportunity to ask God to forgive you.

If you are reading this and you are yet to surrender to Jesus, you better do so quickly before you move into the prayer section. Otherwise you cannot introduce order into your life. If you want to surrender your life to Jesus, pray this prayer: "Lord Jesus, I come before you and confess my sins. Forgive me. O Lord, and cleanse me with your precious blood. Come into my life now. Take control of my life, in Jesus' name. Amen."

PRAYER POINTS

1. O Lord, let my prayer arrow bring results, in Jesus' name.
2. (Use your right hand to cover your two eyes as you pray this prayer with faith): Oh Lord, reveal hidden things to me that will move me forward, in the name of Jesus.
3. Every power that has refused to allow my star to operate, die, in Jesus' name.
4. I recover my stolen stars by fire, in the name of Jesus.
5. I recover my stolen stars by thunder, in the name of Jesus.
6. I reject every evil prophecy, in the name of Jesus.
7. Let the cloud, blocking the sunlight of my stars, be dispersed, in Jesus name.
8. Every pit, dug to swallow my star, be covered by the blood of Jesus.
9. Star demoters, receive the sword of fire, in Jesus name
10. Power of God, move me forward by fire, in the name Jesus
11. I rise above every dark sentence issued against my stars in the name of Jesus.

PUBLICATIONS OF DR. D. K. OLUKOYA

1. 20 Marching Orders To Fulfil Your Destiny
2. 40 Marriages That Must Not Hold
3. 30 Things Anointing Can Do For You
4. 70 Rules of Spiritual Warfare
5. A-Z of Complete Deliverance
6. Be Prepared
7. Bewitchment must die
8. Biblical Principles of Dream Interpretation .
9. Born Great, But Tied Down
10. Breaking Bad Habits
11. Breakthrough Prayers For Business Professionals
12. Brokenness
13. Bringing Down The Power of God
14. Can God?
15. Can God Trust You?
16. Command The Morning
17. Consecration Commitment & Loyalty
18. Contending For The Kingdom
19. Connecting to The God of Breakthroughs
20. Criminals In The House Of God
21. Dealing With Hidden Curses
22. Dealing With Local Satanic Technology
23. Dealing With Satanic Exchange
24. Dealing With The Evil Powers Of Your Father's House
25. Dealing With Tropical Demons
26. Dealing With Unprofitable Roots
27. Dealing With Witchcraft Barbers
28. Deliverance By Fire

YORUBA PUBLICATIONS

Dr. D.K. Olukoya

FRENCH PUBLICATIONS

1. Pluie De Priere
2. EspiritDe Vagabondage
3. En Finir Avec Les Forces Malefiques De La Maison De Ton P ere
4. Quel'envoutementPerisse
5. Frappez I' adversaire Et II Fuira

6. Comment Recevior La Delivrance Du Mari Et Femme DeNuit
7. Cpmment Se Delivrer Soi-meme
8. Povoir Contre Les Terrorites Spiritual
9. Priere De Percees Pour Les Hommes D' affaires
10. PrierJusqu'a Remporter LaVictoire
11. Prieres Violentes Pour Humilier Les Problemes Opiniatres
12. Priere Pour Detruire Les Maladies Et Infirmites
13. Le Combat Spirituel Et Le Foyer
14. Bilan Spirituel Personnel
15. Victoires Sur Les Reves Sataniques
16. Prieres De Comat Contre 70 Espirits Dechanines
17. La Deviation Satanique De La Race Noire
18. Ton Combat Et Ta Strategic
19. Votre Fondement Et Votre Destin
20. Revoquer Les Decrets Malefiques
21. Cantique Des Contiques
22. Le Mauvais Cri Des Idoles